Simply Wait

SIMPLY WAIT

Cultivating Stillness in
the Season of Advent

PAMELA C. HAWKINS

UPPER
ROOM BOOKS®
NASHVILLE

SIMPLY WAIT
Cultivating Stillness in the Season of Advent
Copyright © 2007 by Pamela C. Hawkins
All rights reserved.

Cover and interior design: Studio Haus, Nashville, TN
Cover and interior images: Getty Images

ISBN 978-0-8358-9917-8

To my mother,
Jean Swingle Cunningham,
who has taught me to wait in God's time.

CONTENTS

INTRODUCTION

THE IDEA FOR this book arose from my own experience of contemplative prayer, prayer that finds its home not in busy doing or speaking but in becoming, in being. Several years ago a friend suggested that we attend a one-day Advent retreat in which contemplative prayer was to be a part. I really did not have time to do this—especially during the busy season before Christmas. After all, there were gifts to wrap, school plays to attend, and more church activities than I could fit into my calendar, but my friend persisted and signed us up.

From the moment we arrived, the room set aside for our retreat was bathed in a spirit of quiet and calm. The meeting space was not overdecorated in reds, greens, and golds; Christmas music did not greet us at the door. Instead, in the center of the room stood a small table draped with a plain purple cloth and adorned with a single burning candle. We were welcomed into a hospitable and generous silence. I can still remember the stark impact of that space and silence. I had arrived out of breath from details of a Christmas that had not yet taken place.

In the course of that one day our small group was led through simple prayers, reading of Advent scriptures, and plenty of quiet time in which to imagine how our life with God was being drawn toward Immanuel, God-With-Us. One of the most memorable activities that stirred my imagination was a spiritual exercise of simplicity—the simplicity of a single word.

As we sat in a circle, a basket filled with small pieces of folded paper was passed around. Each piece, we were told, had one word on it. Nothing more. And we were instructed to take one, go to a quiet place in the building, and to sit with that word. We were to let our word sift through our thoughts and over our experiences as we contemplated what meaning it might hold in our life with God and our life with others. We were urged to take time with the word, allowing it to lead us into prayer and memories. We were given almost an hour to do so.

I recall my reaction to these instructions: they could not be correct! How were we to spend so much time with one word? An article, maybe a paragraph, would be worth that much time, but not just a word. We were a literate group, readers and thinkers, people who had taken the time to come apart for this Advent day, and the leader wanted to use our valuable time with a single word.

But I followed the instructions, despite my suspicions that I would soon be bored or distracted from whatever word I drew out of the basket. And as our imposed quiet began, I slowly unfolded my little paper and saw the word in the palm of my hand: Joy. That was it. Joy. Over the next almost-hour, I found myself living with this word in ways that I could not have imagined had others not helped me make room for it that Advent day years ago. Songs came to mind, and faces came to view. Favorite times of day seemed to know the place of joy for me, as did certain childhood memories and vacation snapshots. I found myself wondering about where joy comes from and why it sometimes disappears in an instant. And, in all of this, my thoughts repeatedly returned to God. The time passed by, and the prayers took form—all wrapped up in one little word and one short stretch of minutes spent with the One in whom my word had its home.

In the pages of this Advent resource I hope to offer you—either as an individual or as a member of a group or class—some space in which to also practice simplicity with words. Not just any words will do here but words chosen out of this most holy season of Advent. For each of the four weeks in this season, a single word has been discerned out of the scripture readings assigned for the week from the Revised Common Lectionary. Through a set of weekly guided spiritual practices you are invited to live with an Advent word. Depending on the time you have available each week to use this resource, you may choose to follow all the practices or to select a few that catch your Advent attention most. The practices include

- reflection
- silence
- prayer
- reading scripture
- reading or singing of hymn texts
- Christian service in a waiting world

For each week and word a particular form of prayer from the Christian tradition is described. You may choose to learn or experience some prayer practices that are new to you. I selected these prayers for the way in which they illumine the word of the week and to embody the word within our Advent living. Advent living is what Advent leads us toward: the Word embodied, Immanuel— "the Word became flesh and lived among us" (John 1:14).

I hope these prayers and practices will lead you to slow down and simplify your Advent way of life. May it be a guide into the season—one word at a time.

HOW TO USE THIS BOOK

Participants

This book is designed for individuals, small groups, or classes to use. For small-group use, a guide for leaders is provided in the back of the resource. Although intended as an adult resource, much of the material could be used by or adapted for youth.

Time

The reading and exercises in this resource may be used either of two ways. (1) You can read and reflect a little bit each day of the week (thirty minutes on Day One, ten minutes Days Two–Six, variable times for Day Seven according to the prayer practice). (2) You can read though the entire week's material in a single sitting (approximately an hour), adding time if you choose to follow the Advent prayer practice.

Setting

For individual use, a quiet setting where you can read and reflect with minimal interruption is appropriate. Many people find setting aside the same time each day or week in which to complete this spiritual practice fosters consistency. Putting your reading and reflection materials near a favorite chair or window may enhance the invitation to enter into this Advent time of preparation.

For small groups or classes, activities can be modified for discussion and shared experience (see Guide for Small Groups in the back of the book). Keep the physical setting for small groups simple: a circle of chairs, a single candle, and good lighting so participants can read and write during the conversation. This resource also can be adapted for an Advent retreat with any one or a combination of the weekly themes as a focus.

Materials Needed

Each participant needs a copy of *Simply Wait* in which to journal and make notes, a Bible (any translation), and a journal or other writing material if anyone wants more space than the book provides.

Reading and Preparation

Simply Wait offers material for the four weeks of Advent, beginning with reflection on the first Sunday of Advent and ending with a simple prayer of invocation on Christmas Eve. As mentioned under "Time," materials may be used for daily reflection of thirty minutes on Day One, followed by ten to fifteen minutes each day thereafter, or can be read in one weekly sitting of approximately an hour. Each recommended Prayer Practice, if followed, has its own time frame.

In each week's material you will find:

RESPONDING TO A WORD

Each week begins with a single word that arises out of the four readings assigned from the Revised Common Lectionary. Beginning with a time of silent reflection on the word, the remainder of the week's experiences are also centered on this word, guided by prayer, scripture, hymn texts, and a call to service in a waiting world. It is important to note that if you do not move beyond Day One's set of reflections and prayer but choose to stay in these exercises, your Advent experience may take you right where you need to be. Do not feel pressed to "do it all" if the pace seems more than you desire. Living with the word and your reflections may be enough. The other activities and experiences are offered simply to assist you.

SPACE FOR JOURNALING

Open space is provided in this book for you to journal and make notes when you are invited to reflect. I hope that this will simplify the process for you, having what you need where you need it. You may wish to keep an additional journal or paper nearby if you desire to write more than this book's space permits, but just enough room might be here. At the end of the Advent season, you can look back at your notes and entries to remember how God met you in this season.

INVOCATION AND SILENCE

A prayer of invocation in each chapter points to the word and theme of the week. I urge you to pray this prayer each day during the week, even if you do not return to the other parts of the book on a daily basis. Making room for this little practice each day, paired with a few minutes of silence, can transform your perception and experience of time with God.

REFLECTIONS ON THE WORD

Each week, following the first few pages of material, you will be guided to the four Advent scripture texts designated in the Revised Common Lectionary. You may choose to read them all in one sitting or to read each one on a different day. Note that you will be reflecting on the scriptures after they are read for an Advent Sunday, rather than reading scriptures for the upcoming Sunday. This plan is intentional. The aim is to slow down and not to get ahead of yourselves or ahead of God. If your faith community preaches from the lectionary texts, consider how much better it might be for you to savor and sift through what you have heard each Sunday during the following week.

After each reading a brief reflection on and out of the Word is offered, concluding with a question or activity for your consideration. Again I urge you to take your time with one or all of these and to respond as the Spirit leads you in the space provided or elsewhere.

HYMN TO READ OR SING

The Advent hymns selected point to the theme and word of the week. Whether read or sung by individuals or groups, these hymn texts create an additional window of prayer into the season. Also they represent a historical dimension to this resource, with authorship spanning over two hundred years of Christian reflection on the meaning of Christ's promised coming—in the past and today.

BENEDICTION

A brief benediction closes each Day One. These simple blessings may be whispered to God after a time of prayer, before the end of a day, or at the conclusion of a gathering.

WEEKLY ADVENT PRAYER PRACTICE

You are invited to learn or review a form of prayer that fits well into the season of Advent. A particular prayer practice is presented each week with brief instruction. Each requires a different amount of time to practice from a few minutes to a few hours.

BEFORE YOU BEGIN

Before you turn the page and begin this journey into Advent, find a quiet place to go each time you use this prayer and guide book. As best as you can, try to set aside the looming distractions of the season, all the lists and longings that begin to grow as soon as Christmas appears on the calendar. Instead, as you hold this book in your hands, create space for God who invites you to choose a different way of living this year, a way of prayer and reflection about the words and days that stretch before you with slow and deliberate holy design.

These next few weeks can be unwrapped as pure gifts from God who invites you to prepare carefully for the coming of Christ, the birth of God's most precious gift to the world. The scripture texts presented here for reading and reflection have, for centuries, brought light to the dark places of human hearts and night skies. The practice of prayer has, through the ages, brought breath and calm to a laboring world groaning for newness to be born among us. And a single Word, made flesh, has brought God to us, God-With-Us, Immanuel.

Begin.

ANTICIPATION

Wait with this word for awhile before you turn the page. Let *Anticipation* settle into your thoughts. Let this word soak into your life. Let it spread across your imagination as you look toward Christmas. Do not hurry. Wait. And when you have taken some time with this word, turn the page.

DAY ONE
Responding to the Word *Anticipation*

What is your first reaction to this word?

Describe your most recent experience of *anticipation*.
Be as specific as possible.

What memories or stories from past Advent and Christmas
seasons does this word, *anticipation*, call forth from your life?

What might God desire that you *anticipate* in the gift
of these days and weeks that lead toward Christmas?

INVOCATION

Holy Anticipation,
that breathtaking space in-between
what has been, what is, what is-to-come.
Where winter dreams reveal secret longings
and winged angels announce the coming of Love.
You draw us to the edge of Advent possibility
like the song of angels drawing shepherds—
eyes wide and breath held—
waiting, watching.
Come, settle into our living for awhile
and do not let us settle for too little.
Amen.

SILENCE

REFLECTION ON *ANTICIPATION*

As we entered the sanctuary, it was almost time for the Advent Service of Lessons and Carols to begin. After friends made room for us on their crowded pew, we sat down just as the choir moved into place for the processional hymn. When I looked up, I noticed a man sitting alone in the choir loft. He was middle-aged, dressed in a choir robe, and was leaning forward in an odd posture. At first, I thought he had arrived too late to join the rest of the choir at the back of the church. He must have decided just to hurry to his seat.

Yet as I watched him more closely, there was nothing rushed about him, but rather the contrary—he seemed calm and unhurried. This man sat very still, almost strangely so—eyes straight ahead, jaw thrust up, neck taut—holding still as though he anticipated something was about to happen.

Then suddenly he stood up, as if he had heard some cue inaudible to the rest of us. And he broke into a smile that lit up his whole person, a smile like we see on someone who has received wonderful news; yet he stood there alone, no one near him, leaning over the choir screen and into the open space beyond him.

That was when I realized the man was blind. He had not arrived late but had been waiting right where he needed to be, probably where he waited often. He had been listening for the sound of readiness, a sound he had attuned his ears to hear. He was anticipating with his whole being that first sound of movement and music from a distance. He was leaning into the Advent space of God's gathered people, poised and ready, and when he heard what he had been waiting for, he was moved to joy.

May we be so poised this Advent. May we learn to wait well, expectations high, stretching toward God's people. May we grow in anticipation of what the coming of Christ can mean for the waiting world. May we seek and find our place in the unfolding story of Christ.

HYMN OF ANTICIPATION

Sing or read the words of this Advent hymn. Attend to the words carefully. How do they stir up a sense of anticipation for this season?

PEOPLE, LOOK EAST

People, look east.
The time is near of the crowning of the year.
Make your house fair as you are able,
trim the hearth and set the table.
People, look east and sing today:
Love, the Guest, is on the way.

Furrows, be glad.
Though earth is bare, one more seed is planted there.
Give up your strength the seed to nourish,
that in course the flower may flourish.
People, look east and sing today:
Love, the Rose, is on the way.

Stars, keep the watch.
When night is dim, one more light the bowl shall brim,
shining beyond the frosty weather,
bright as sun and moon together.
People, look east and sing today:
Love, the Star, is on the way.

Angels announce with shouts of mirth
him who brings new life to earth.
Set every peak and valley humming
with the word, the Lord is coming.
People, look east and sing today:
Love, the Lord, is on the way.

—Eleanor Farjeon

BENEDICTION

Wait for the Lord. Set your face toward the East and your heart toward the One who is to come. Wait for the Lord. Anticipate his presence, for he is very near and he is coming to make all things new. Amen.

DAY TWO

Read Isaiah 2:1-5.

"IN DAYS TO COME . . . ," begins the prophet, painting the first strokes of a promised future for the people of God. Then, in a poetic series of *shall* after *shall* after *shall*, he broadens the vision of what life with God can mean for a people who together come to the house of the Lord.

In the Advent "days to come" when will you next enter God's house for worship? What do you anticipate experiencing there? What will you see? What will you hear? How do you anticipate meeting God in the experience of worship this Advent season? Sit down with a calendar and mark the times you will be in God's house this season. Begin to prepare your heart and life in prayer for those times when you will enter the house of the Lord.

Your reflections—

DAY THREE

Read Psalm 122.

FOR THE PSALMIST the gift of peace is the gift most desired for "relatives and friends." Is not peace still our hearts' desire? Can we stretch our imaginations around such an Advent possibility—that somewhere in the world where peace is longed for it could become a reality? In this season of gift making and gift giving, could we begin to anticipate through prayer and action what the gift of peace around the world, across the city, and in our homes could look like?

Take time with this psalm and stretch your imagination around a particular relationship, a specific circumstance, or a named place in the world where we could anticipate how God's gift of peace might change everything. Use a globe, a newspaper, or a photograph—whatever will help you name and remember the ones in need of peace. On behalf of the ones who come to your mind, write a prayer to Christ, the Prince of Peace.

Your reflections—

DAY FOUR
Read Romans 13:11-14.

IN THIS LETTER Paul urges us to live the Christian life now, in this time and place! Live like people who believe and anticipate that Christ has come, is coming, and will come again! Live a life that stands out against the ways of the world.

Do our Advent lives stand up against the ways of the world? Are we already so consumed with Christmas, even now in the first week of Advent, that we neglect taking time to live fully into the meaning and experience of the coming of Christ? It is not yet Christmas but Advent. This is a season in which we have time to anticipate the full story and meaning of Immanuel—God-With-Us—if we will take that time and use it well.

Take a walk through your home, room by room, and say an Advent blessing in each space, something simple like "O come, O come, Immanuel" or "Come, Lord Jesus." Take your time, imagining how you will live in this time and place over the next few weeks in ways that could help you not hurry to Christmas.

Your reflections—

DAY FIVE
Read Matthew 24:36-44.

HERE JESUS TELLS how, with the help of God, Noah anticipated and made ready for the flood, while others ignored God and lost their lives. Perhaps the others were too consumed with the ways of the world, distracted by their own interests. But Noah had learned to pay attention to what mattered to God; and what mattered to God were the ones who mattered to Noah.

We are entering a season when much of the world will be attracted by glitter and glimmer, but we are invited to anticipate with God what really matters in our lives. Take pen and paper to a quiet place where you can be alone for awhile: a place with few distractions. Begin a list of the people you love, all those persons who are dear to you, the ones you want to carry in your heart this season. Keep this list over the whole Advent season; add to it anytime. Be satisfied with remembering these individuals in prayer and thought for now.

Your reflections—

DAY SIX
The Waiting World

PLAN TO WATCH a report of world and national news at least once this week. List the main stories as the program moves through them, and when the program is over, retreat to a quiet place. Look over the list of stories. How can deepened anticipation for God's desired outcome play a role in these situations?

Sit prayerfully with these stories and consider how the practice of faithful anticipation might bring healing to a waiting world. How could anticipation move into action?

Your reflections—

DAY SEVEN

Praying in Anticipation

My soul waits for the Lord,
more than those who watch for the morning,
more than those who watch for the morning.

—Psalm 130:6

VIGILS

Vigil, at its most basic, means an act of wakefulness or watching. In the context of prayer, *vigil* is most often associated with an extended, intentional time of prayer, often at night or before a holy day or occasion.

Some congregations schedule and practice prayer vigils during times of communal discernment about new ministries, in difficult times, or pending significant decisions; and often vigils are observed in a community for specific social action or justice concerns. There are faith communities that observe a night office (an *office* is a practice of daily set prayer) of vigils, in which the whole community awakens and gathers before dawn to "keep watch" with God for a period of prayer and meditation on God's Word. Many Christians also observe an occasional personal practice of vigils, by choosing a night to stay awake in prayer when their spirit is troubled or when concern for a person or a circumstance weighs heavily on their heart. They pray and meditate on scripture until God's dawning light breaks on a new day.

In Advent the prayer practice of vigils is one that well illumines the meaning of anticipation. To be in prayer with God while waiting for the darkness to turn toward light is to be watchful with God, to be full of anticipation for what God is doing in the world as we turn toward the promised birth of the Christ child. Although many prayer practices foster growth in our ability to wait for and anticipate God's gracious action in our lives, the practice of vigils invites us into a real-time experience. We wait for and anticipate God's action in the arrival of dawn. Vigils requires waiting in the dark, fully awake, fully present, and fully prayerful. It requires sacrifice of routine for the purpose of change. The practice of vigils represents the very kind of prayerful waiting and sacrifice required of Joseph and Mary on the night of Jesus' birth.

As one way into prayer during Advent, you are invited to enter into the prayer practice of vigils. A brief guide for individual practice follows. You may adapt it for use in a group or community. May this way of prayer enrich your experience of Advent anticipation.

A GUIDE TO THE PRACTICE OF VIGILS

Vigils is most often associated with a communal practice of prayer, but it also offers a deeply personal time with God when experienced as an individual practice. The following guide is simply one way for you to try this practice alone, but it can be easily adapted to use with a friend or group.

Vigils is a predawn prayer, beginning at least an hour before sunrise. Two full hours are recommended for this practice, but you may desire more or less time according to your discernment.

Choose the night/morning for this prayer time and mark it on your calendar. Find out from the newspaper, Internet, or local weather report the approximate time of sunrise for the morning so that you can set your clock in time to be in the prayer space at least one full hour before sunrise. Choose your setting for prayer, preferably a space with windows so that the morning light may enter. Place a candle in the room, and be sure to have a source of low light by which to read scripture and prayers. Select and mark the texts for reading and meditation so that you can find them easily. You may wish to use the lectionary readings for the week (Isa. 2:1-5; Ps. 122; Rom. 13:11-14; Matt. 24:36-44). Alternatively, choose several psalms with special meaning for you.

When it is time for prayer, light your candle and sink into the quiet. Spend at least fifteen minutes in silent prayer, then read aloud one of the scriptures and let enough silence follow so that you can meditate on what God needs you to hear in the text and in the morning. Move to the next reading and do the same until all the scriptures have been read and prayed while the day's light breaks in. Go slowly and leave ample silence for prayer and reflection. Resist any conversation if you are with others. Focus your attention and heart upon God's dawning presence with you in the day ahead.

After the readings and silence, invite prayers for the day—read or spoken—for others, for blessings, for concerns, for the world, and for the season. After more silent prayer, wait and watch in the dawn. Make room for the light to filter in and, once sunrise has passed and you have been in prayer for at least two full hours, prepare to move into the rest of your day and "Go in peace."

HOPE

Wait with this word for awhile before you turn the page. Let *Hope* settle into your thoughts. Let this word soak into your life. Let it spread across your imagination as you look toward Christmas. Do not hurry. Wait. And when you have taken some time with this word, turn the page.

DAY ONE

Responding to the Word *Hope*

What is your first reaction to this word?

Hope.

Describe your most recent experience of *hope*.
Be as specific as possible.

What memories or stories from past Advent and Christmas
seasons does this word, *hope*, call forth from your life?

What might God desire that you *hope* for in the gift of these days
and weeks that lead us toward Christmas?

INVOCATION

O Hope,
aperture of God's expansive view;
prism through which all true Light breaks,
illuminating paths and patterns,
ways and wanderers.
Refract our shortsightedness
that we may look to the East with distance vision
and find our Advent way.
Come, O Hope,
focus our blurred
and distracted sight
that we might see clearly the One who is coming.
Amen.

SILENCE

REFLECTION ON *HOPE*

Hope. Perhaps no other word better illumines the Advent story. Hope that Mary would say Yes! Hope that Joseph would not reject her upon hearing the news of her pregnancy. Hope that their long journey to Bethlehem would bring no harm. Hope that the bright star overhead would bring only good.

Parents hope for room in an inn. Shepherds hope for good news of a birth in a manger. Angels hope for peace in human hearts. Advent could not be Advent without hope. Not at the first and not today, for without the borning cry of hope, the world could descend into deadening discouragement.

Hope opens something in the human heart. Like shutters slowly parting to admit a winter dawn, hope permits strands of light to make their way to us, even when we still stand in cold darkness; but hope also reveals a landscape beyond us into which we can live and move and have our being. With hope, closely held interior thoughts are gently turned outward; deep desires, perhaps long hidden in secret corners of our heart, might be lifted up to the light. At times, hope peels back the edges of our imagination to free what waits underneath—a changed life, a new resolve, a yes pregnant with possibility. In other moments hope dares us to unfold a layer of desire—for relationship, for clarity, for courage.

In the stories and season of Advent, God opens everything to us through hope born of expectation—expectation that Christ is coming to make all things new. And in the coming of Christ we find the coming of hope, made real in time, space, and flesh.

May you, like an expectant parent, use these days and nights prayerfully hoping for what is to come. May you live through the scriptures of this season, in which the light of God's hope breaks in on a waiting world to illumine the landscape in which we live and move and have our being.

HYMN OF HOPE

Sing or read the words of this Advent hymn. Attend to the words carefully. How do they stir up a sense of hope for this season?

COME, THOU LONG-EXPECTED JESUS

Come, thou long-expected Jesus,
born to set thy people free;
from our fears and sins release us,
let us find our rest in thee.
Israel's strength and consolation,
hope of all the earth thou art;
dear desire of every nation,
joy of every longing heart.

Born thy people to deliver,
born a child and yet a King,
born to reign in us forever,
now thy gracious kingdom bring.
By thine own eternal spirit rule in all our hearts alone;
by thine all sufficient merit,
raise us to thy glorious throne.

—Charles Wesley

BENEDICTION

Hope in the Lord. May night give way to morning; may darkness break open to light; may you make room for Christ. Hope in the Lord, for he is coming to make all things new. Amen.

DAY TWO

Read Isaiah 11:1-10.

"A SHOOT SHALL come out from the stump of Jesse," the reading begins. A sure sign of hope is a sign of life where at first there seems to be no life. As winter leaves a sparse and barren landscape, spring brings rooted signs of newness in the unfolding of each day. The prophet Isaiah understood this image of hope for the imaginations of God's people.

As you sit with this psalm from Isaiah, write down the names of three people in your life who come to mind as you think of persons who need a sign of hope. For what do they hope? What "shoot" or "bud" would be a sign of life to them and to those who love them? Pray for each one by name, and in your prayer, speak aloud their individual hope. Plant these prayers in the winter soil of Advent and release them to God, asking God to tend to them through this season and beyond.

Your reflections—

DAY THREE

Read Psalm 72:1-7, 18-19.

THE PSALMIST PRAYS to God for the establishment of a kingdom in which justice, righteousness, and peace are realized. Here is a word about God's hope for creation, a God-shaped hope where love for neighbor flourishes.

Get a map of your city and spread it out on a table. Look over the different parts of town and pray for each section, the ones in which you know neighbors and the ones where you do not. Pay attention to parts of your city where issues of justice and fairness need your attention. Sit with this map for awhile and pray for the establishment of God's reign on earth and for how, this Advent, you can be an instrument in the coming of that reign where hope resides.

Your reflections—

DAY FOUR

Read Romans 15:4-13.

IN THIS PASSAGE from Paul there is no question about the role of hope in the Christian life. The reading ends with these words: "May the God of hope fill you with all joy and peace in believing, so that you may abound in hope by the power of the Holy Spirit." And just a few lines before this, in verse 4, Paul teaches the people that one sure source of hope is scripture, God's holy Word.

Is there a story or passage from scripture that comes to mind when you think about hope? If so, take time to recall it. If you know where the passage is located, mark its place in your Bible. If you do now know where to find it, simply mark its place in your memory by recalling all that you can about it.

If no scripture comes to mind for you, ask a close friend or family member for a suggestion of scripture that speaks of hope. Invite the person to share that passage with you.

Your reflections—

DAY FIVE

Read Matthew 3:1-12.

A ROUGH AND wild John the Baptist seems to interrupt Advent's gentler story. But the way of the Lord, the path for Jesus, had to be prepared so that people did not miss what God was doing right before their eyes. John's life was full of sacrifice. He lived and died so that Jesus could bring hope into the world. John lived and died so that God's Word could be fulfilled.

Who prepared a way for you to follow Jesus? Who taught you about the Bible? Where did you learn about prayer? What is your earliest memory of worship or Sunday school? Write down the names of people who helped prepare a way for you to grow in your faith and in your hope in God. Then simply give God thanks for these persons in your life.

Your reflections—

DAY SIX
The Waiting World

IF A YOUNG couple expecting their first child came to your community tonight with no money, no place to live, and no medical care, where they could stay? What hope does your community offer for such a need? Take time to find out what services are provided in your community. Become informed about these services and choose a way to support one of these services with your time, resources, and prayers. Help "prepare the way" of hope in a waiting world.

Your reflections—

DAY SEVEN

Praying in Hope

By awesome deeds you answer us with deliverance,
O God of our salvation;
you are the hope of all the ends of the earth
and of the farthest seas.
—Psalm 65:5

DAILY EXAMEN

One classic prayer practice is called the *daily examen*. Nothing about this form of prayer hides behind its name: it is a *daily* prayer by which to *examine* life with God. What can be more hopeful than a prayer by which we honestly bring before God the ins, outs, ups, and downs of a day, and then learn to release them all to the One who already knows us inside out. By such a practice, each new day begins in the hope for new life.

A daily examen prayer is usually practiced just before going to bed. There are many different models and forms for this kind of prayer, but in each of them we are invited to take time to remember the past day—what we thought, did, and felt—and with a simple set of questions, examine our responses before and with God. Essentially a prayer of examen makes room for an honest accounting of the day: where we were strong in faith and where we were weak or neglectful. A prayer of examen allows us to scan back over the day with an eye to both the moments when our thoughts or actions were pleasing to God and those when our responses were less faithful.

To live into God's hope requires learning to trust the ways of God, sharing with God a full and honest relationship. One of God's ways is the way of hope—making all things new in any time or place. A prayer of examen allows us to set our entire day before God, including the parts that did not delight God, and to entrust the past day to God so that in the morning, in the new day, we can begin again in God's merciful hope. May this way of prayer release us into Advent hopefulness.

A GUIDE TO THE PRACTICE OF A DAILY EXAMEN

As mentioned, a daily examen is prayed just before going to sleep. It may take five minutes or twenty, depending on how much time you choose to spend in the practice. The following guide, based on my own practice, may be adapted to the language and questions of your own life. This model rarely takes more than ten minutes for me to complete and often even less time.

To begin, choose the night when you will make room for the practice. Go about all usual bedtime routines so that once ready to retire, no other tasks will need your attention. Then move to your bed or chair and ask yourself the following questions, sitting with each one for a few minutes as you sift through the day's events. Make mental notes or, if you journal, feel free to do so.

- *When in this day was I aware of God's presence?* (Be specific as you remember.)
- *When were my actions and choices in this day pleasing to God?*
- *When were my actions and choices not pleasing to God?*

Now release into God's care all of the day, the ways in which your life delighted God and the ways in which you may have missed the mark of God's delight. Imagine turning all over to God so that you can rest in God and rest in hope that the next day will provide new opportunities to awaken to God's presence and to begin again the life of faith. Ask for God's help in rest and waking. Rest.

Clearly, a daily examen is a very personal prayer. It is an individual prayer, most often practiced in solitude, but a group can practice this prayer in community. A group, class, or community can learn the practice together and make a commitment to one another to practice it each night over a period of time. For example, this prayer could be learned and then prayed for the remainder of Advent and through the Christmas season, or a small group could go on retreat and commit to practicing the examen each night of the retreat.

PATIENCE

Wait with this word for awhile before you turn the page. Let *Patience* settle into your thoughts. Let this word soak into your life. Let it spread across your imagination as you look toward Christmas. Do not hurry. Wait. And when you have taken some time with this word, turn the page.

DAY ONE

Responding to the Word *Patience*

What is your first reaction to this word?

Describe your most recent experience of *patience*.
Be as specific as possible.

What memories or stories from past Advent and Christmas
seasons does this word, *patience*, call forth from your life?

What might God desire that you *hope* for in the gift of these days
and weeks that lead us toward Christmas?

INVOCATION

Holy Patience,
that deep, calm resistance
against the riptide of the season's hurry,
while swell upon swell of Christmas
laps at every edge of our lives,
you call us to an Advent way of living;
deep calling to deep,
love bearing love,
Word becoming flesh.
Slow, labored, beloved Patience,
come, teach us to trust in Advent's buoyancy;
suspend us, outstretched, for the coming of Christ.
Amen.

SILENCE

REFLECTION ON *PATIENCE*

Waiting for Christmas is like waiting for a star to fall. We know it will come, streaking across our lives with promised Light, but we can grow weary from the Advent strain of waiting.

In the early years of our marriage, my husband and I lived near the ocean. One favorite winter tradition was to pack a picnic dinner and head to the beach so that we could be there as day turned to night. Wrapped in our winter coats, hats, and gloves, we sat on an old sleeping bag and began to watch the sky as the stars made their light known. First one, then another, then a third would come into focus, and finally whole constellations competed for our attention. It was always a holy sight to behold.

Once the frozen background of the winter night's sky darkened just enough, we began our watch for falling stars. "There!" It seemed like Ray always saw the first one. I would look in the direction he pointed but often too late to see. My shoulders tightened, my neck strained, and I tried to keep from blinking so that I wouldn't miss the next shooting point of light. Sometimes I realized I was holding my breath, as if that would help; as if suspension of my own breathing could in some way suspend the movement of the heavens and allow me to see more clearly. But as soon as I looked in one direction, Ray would cry out again, "Look, there's another one"; and no sooner would I turn his way than the stream of light was gone.

Still, with practice, I learned that if I just kept looking, patiently, I would almost always find a falling star. Over time I learned from friends who had lived by the ocean longer than I that the likelihood of finding a falling star was greater in certain seasons of the year or in particular quadrants of the sky. I learned that if I lay down with my head propped just right on Ray's knee, I could wait longer and watch better. I just had to let patience, desire, and practice teach me to be present to what was to come.

So it is with Advent and patience. As we begin to watch impatiently for the Light of Christmas, we have been given this stretch of time and space of Advent. Here we are invited to grow in patience and to position our lives so that we do not miss what God is doing in the wide expanse of the world.

May we slow down, spread out our whole lives before God, and practice patient watching for where the light of God is falling. May we catch a glimpse of this holy light, of the lives and places in the world that need our attention and are illumined by God's radiance so as to draw us near. May we all settle into Advent with a deep desire to see and attend to what matters to God.

HYMN OF PATIENCE

Sing or read the words of this Advent hymn. Attend to the words carefully. How do they stir up a sense of patience for this season?

I WANT TO WALK AS A CHILD OF THE LIGHT

I want to walk as a child of the light.
I want to follow Jesus.
God set the stars to give light to the world.
The star of my life is Jesus.

[refrain]
In him there is no darkness at all.
The night and the day are both alike.
The Lamb is the light of the city of God.
Shine in my heart, Lord Jesus.

I want to see the brightness of God.
I want to look at Jesus.
Clear Sun of Righteousness, shine on my path,
and show me the way to the Father. [refrain]

I'm looking for the coming of Christ.
I want to be with Jesus.
When we have run with patience the race,
we shall know the joy of Jesus. [refrain]

—Kathleen Thomerson

BENEDICTION

May the Holy Spirit fall upon you. Like a falling star, trailing across the dawns and dusks of your Advent living, may the Spirit mark you with light and point the way toward God-With-Us. Be patient, draw close, for the Lord is very near. Amen.

DAY TWO
Read Isaiah 35:1-10.

THE PROPHET CALLS upon the deep imagination of God's people to watch patiently for signs of change. In the dark season of exile, life signs have seemed dormant, dried up, and closed off. But in a new season of light, like spring after winter, life signs will break through for all who have held fast patiently through the darkness. This is a text about what will be, about what shall be, for those who patiently watch for and trust God's restoring care for them, even after a bitter, hard season.

Reread this passage from Isaiah, but do so slowly, patiently. Take your time with the text and read it with expectation that it holds a word of life for you to see, like the first crocus bloom in early spring. Which particular verse catches your attention? Write it down and sit with that one verse or part of a verse. Be patient. What does it call forth from you? What does it touch in your life? Simply be in patient prayer.

Your reflections—

DAY THREE

Read Luke 1:47-55.

OUT OF A YOUNG life tumble words of inordinate wisdom. Who could have predicted this kind of meaningful, dangerous language from a powerless girl of no means? On the face of her life, we would have expected a different kind of song—a child's song, a playful song, maybe the first notes of a lullaby; but not this kind of song, full of radical, upside-down prophecy meant to awaken rather than to lull to sleep. The world was already asleep to what God had in mind. That was the problem. The song needed to be a song of impatience about a world that even a child could see needed to be turned topsy-turvy.

Read the passage again, this time from the perspective of a child or youth of your community who is in need or lives on the margin in some way. How might Mary's song speak for this child or youth? In what ways might systems be turned upside down in order for this young person to be blessed by a different life? How might you grow in your impatience with systems that wound and neglect children? Is there a prophetic word or action that you could claim on their behalf?

Your reflections—

DAY FOUR

Read James 5:7-10.

"BE PATIENT, THEREFORE, beloved, until the coming of the Lord." In this letter the author urges the church to whom he writes to practice being patient with one another in their life together. How easy it is, especially in busy, difficult, and stressful times, to resort to criticism and gossip about people around us, even within the church. Yet as the church, we are called to set an example of holy patience with one another.

Take time to reflect on your own faith community. Are you aware of circumstances where friction, tension, or criticism exist? Do you feel any degree of judgmentalism toward persons, or have you recently grumbled about anyone? Pray for patience with these circumstances or individuals. Ask for God's help in becoming more patient, merciful, and compassionate.

Your reflections—

D𝒜Y FIVE
Read Matthew 11:2-11.

JOHN IS IN prison. He can no longer preach to the crowds or baptize the streams of people who believe that the reign of God is coming near. He is set apart and isolated, and now his followers and friends must prepare the way of the Lord or abandon the task and go on with their everyday lives. So John must wait, patiently, for a word from his friends about whether or not Jesus is the one for whom they have been searching. John can do nothing now but wait on his friends to bring a good word to him about Jesus.

Who in this season is waiting for a good word from you? Who comes to mind among your family, friends, coworkers, or others as set apart by fear, worry, stress, loneliness, anger, self-judgment, or other isolating life conditions? Sit quietly and patiently as you make a list of people you know who need you to bring them a good word, a piece of the good news of God's love for them. Take your time with this process. Write down a name, and then that individual's need (is it encouragement, presence, listening, forgiveness, other?). What good word can you bring each person? Can you go and tell these individuals that word sometime during the Advent season?

Your reflections—

DAY SIX
The Waiting World

WHERE IN THE world are individuals and groups patiently waiting for help from God's people? Where in the world are orphaned children, widows and widowers, people imprisoned or displaced, starving or terrified, who can only wait patiently for someone to take notice of their struggle to stay alive?

Get a newspaper or magazine or go to the Internet and browse for a story from the world community where someone or some group is waiting for and in need of attention and action according to the good news of Jesus. Take action; do something; start somewhere to make their situation known and to bring them a piece of God's good word.

Your reflections—

DAY SEVEN

Praying Patiently

I waited patiently for the LORD;
he inclined to me and heard my cry.
—Psalm 40:1

THE JESUS PRAYER

The Jesus Prayer, often called a "prayer of the heart," is ancient. It best unfolds through patient repetition. It is a short prayer, which, like many small things of God, can be taken for granted until given a chance: like the yes from a teenage girl or the first breath of a tiny, newborn baby. It is, therefore, a splendid prayer for Advent.

The Jesus Prayer has a rich history. You can find many books and articles about this little prayer if you want to know how it came to be and to be practiced through the centuries. Typically in these readings various versions of the prayer that have been prayed through the life of the church will be presented (see Resources at the back of this book). For example, in the most basic English form, the Jesus Prayer has become known as "Lord, have mercy" and in its longest form as "Lord Jesus Christ, Son of the living God, have mercy on me, a sinner." In other versions the name of Jesus and the petition for mercy are prayed in various combinations, such as, "Jesus Christ, have mercy on me" or "Lord Jesus, have mercy" or even a simple "Lord, mercy." But the heart of the prayer is not revealed in its history or in any particular combination of words prayed; the heart of the prayer is revealed through its patient praying.

The Jesus Prayer gets to the heart of our need before God. It hides behind nothing and represents everything that we are before God. Short and to-the-point, it comes to life in us not through wordy, complicated construction but through patient, repeated simplicity. For centuries spiritual guides have instructed seekers to say this little prayer over and over again throughout their day, beginning with small sets of repetition while doing tasks like tending a garden, sweeping a floor, or, more currently, sitting in traffic, and then expanding its use over time so that it might become a means by which we "pray without ceasing" (1 Thess. 5:17). Although at first such a repetitive practice can feel awkward and odd, people who stay with this prayer find that over time it becomes a source of deep comfort and rhythm that arises from the heart, connecting them with the Source of life always present to us.

Perhaps this Advent will be a time when the simple rhythm of an unhurried prayer can be a gift for you. The directions that follow are intended to introduce or reintroduce you to the Jesus Prayer. May this little prayer of the heart guide you into Advent patience and gentleness with yourself and with others.

A GUIDE TO THE PRACTICE OF THE JESUS PRAYER

As with a daily examen, the Jesus Prayer is typically an individual prayer. But as noted before, a prayer like this can also be practiced by a group that might covenant together to learn and practice it for a time and then to share their experiences with it. As with any form of prayer, some people will find this prayer helpful, while others will not. Only through practical experience can you know whether it offers a prayerful space for you.

Unlike many other prayer forms, the Jesus Prayer is not a prayer for sitting or lying still. This is a prayer you can take into activity—standing, walking, driving, digging, cleaning, and more. This prayer may be best suited to the action-soaked and activity-weighted ways of our culture, especially of our pre-Christmas way of life. Therefore, in order to try out this little prayer, you will not need to carve out or leave behind any tasks in your schedule but rather plan to carry the Jesus Prayer into your busy routine.

First, choose the wording that attracts you. Resist overanalyzing your choice. You can change it at any time. You might begin with "Lord Jesus Christ, have mercy on me"; "Jesus Christ, have mercy"; or a longer wording that touches your heart, such as, "Jesus

Christ, have mercy on me, a sinner." Practicing a short version may be easiest in the beginning.

Once you have chosen the wording, simply say it right away in five slowly-paced repetitions. Get a feel for the prayer's rhythm.

Now choose an activity or daily practice already in your schedule at least twice a day. This can be something like brushing your teeth, checking your e-mail, sitting at a red light, walking the dog, filling the dishwasher, leaving your office to attend a meeting—any daily experience that you repeat at least once. Then write out a reminder to take with you or stick on a mirror, computer, door frame, or dashboard to remind you to say the Jesus Prayer five times when the designated activity begins. Each time you attend to this daily activity, say the Jesus Prayer five times again. Do this for a few days.

Next, expand your repetitions to ten. Live with the Jesus Prayer. Experiment with other daily activities where you could add the practice.

Live in the Advent light of Christ's unceasing mercy.

OBEDIENCE

Wait with this word for awhile before you turn the page. Let *Obedience* settle into your thoughts. Let this word soak into your life. Let it spread across your imagination as you look toward Christmas. Do not hurry. Wait. And when you have taken some time with this word, turn the page.

DAY ONE

Responding to the Word *Obedience*

What is your first reaction to this word?

Describe your most recent experience of *obedience*.
Be as specific as possible.

What memories or stories from past Advent and Christmas
seasons does this word, *obedience*, call forth from your life?

How might God desire you to practice *obedience* in these days
and weeks that lead toward Christmas?

INVOCATION

Holy Obedience,
companion of trust,
enemy of fear;
undesired yet longed for;
resistible but irreplaceable.
You who cause ears to turn deadly deaf,
and, at once,
bring life to its grateful knees.
Come, O Obedience,
join us with the angels to listen for God's Advent
that we may hear our way.
Amen.

SILENCE

REFLECTION ON *OBEDIENCE*

A tree grows in our backyard that is like no other tree. Were it not for winter, I might not see this tree for what it has become. In most seasons the trunk and branches are all but hidden behind a patch-work quilt of leaf and light. But in late autumn the distinctive form of the tree begins to be laid bare, revealing a life story to anyone who will pay attention.

The tree is tall, like most trees around it. At the trunk's widest girth, it is still narrow, and without strain I can put my arms around its trunk. With effort, I can shade my eyes against the winter sun, arch my neck, and look up to where its long, tapered fingertip branches seem to scrape the clouds. At the ground where the gray-brown trunk erupts from the soil, this tree looks like all the others in our yard—reaching arrow-straight toward the sky.

But once its leaves have surrendered to autumn's final chill, the light and clarity of winter reveal evidence of a different life lived in this one tree. Halfway up its height, a curve begins—not a slight curve like a sliver of moon but a strong, clear curve like a child's hand cupped around some secret treasure. And then, after bending out and around and up for the length of at least twelve feet, the trunk grows straight again as if this peculiar detour had never appeared.

I can never know what set this tree off course; whether injury or disease in its trunk forced it to grow crooked for survival. Perhaps other trees, more mature and full of themselves, cast too great a shadow for this lone tree to easily find what it needed to live. But I do know that this tree followed the only path for which it was created, and that it did so by seeking and following the life source that is light.

Something along the way caught the attention of this tree, and for its life's sake, it obeyed the Creator's nudge and tug. Whatever pulled and called it into this unique curve, whatever it "listened" to deep inside, may have saved its life at one time. And now, when I see this tree during winter, I am reminded of how obedience to the Creator is really about turning toward the light and voice of God for life's sake.

May we live into the remainder of Advent attuned to the Creator's desires for our lives. May we seek times of Advent solitude, silence and prayer in which we bare our unique soul before the One who formed us to listen for guidance about who we are called to become. May we seek the light of God in Jesus Christ day by day, bending and turning toward Christ even if it makes us stand out from the Christmas crowds. May we learn to listen, in our own deep places for the voice of the One who loves us beyond measure.

HYMN OF OBEDIENCE

Sing or read the words of this Advent hymn. Attend to the words carefully. How do they stir up a sense of obedience for this season?

HAIL TO THE LORD'S ANOINTED

Hail to the Lord's Anointed, great David's greater Son!
Hail in the time appointed, his reign on earth begun!
He comes to break oppression, to set the captive free;
to take away transgression, and rule in equity.

He comes with succor speedy to those who suffer wrong;
to help the poor and needy, and bid the weak be strong;
to give them songs for sighing, their darkness turn to light,
whose souls, condemned and dying, are precious in his sight.

He shall come down like showers upon the fruitful earth;
love, joy, and hope, like flowers, spring in his path to birth.
Before him, on the mountains, shall peace, the herald go,
and righteousness, in fountains, from hill to valley flow.

To him shall prayers unceasing and daily vows ascend;
his kingdom still increasing, a kingdom without end.
The tide of time shall never his covenant remove;
his name shall stand for ever; that name to us is love.
—James Montgomery

BENEDICTION

Listen, for the Lord is very near! May the sound of his voice draw you closer and closer in obedient love—coming and going, waiting and watching, now and forever. Amen.

DAY TWO
Read Isaiah 7:10-16.

OBEDIENCE REQUIRES courage. At a time in which God's people were in need of courage and were feeling alone in an uncertain world, Isaiah gave them a sign that they were not alone. Immanuel, God-With-Us, who called them to be an obedient people, also promised to be a very present help to them in times of trouble if only they would have eyes to see. What signs in these weeks of Advent point you to the presence of God in your life? Where have you seen God-With-Us in the past week? How could you point someone you love toward God-With-Us before this day is done? Write down the signs and circumstances that come to mind and hold them in prayer.

Your reflections—

DAY THREE

Read Psalm 80:1-7, 17-19.

As a shepherd expects a flock to obey his voice, so God expects God's people to do the same. When the flock becomes distracted, it turns away from the shepherd, wandering into dangerous territory and risking life. The psalmist calls upon God the Shepherd to save the wandering flock of Israel, to restore the people to the divine tender care and guidance, and in return the people are expected to obey the voice of God, never again to turn away.

What is distracting your attention this season in ways that make it hard to attend to God's desires for your life? What has caught your eye that competes for God's attention? Take a piece of paper and sketch some of the distractions, or go through a magazine or newspaper and cut out pictures of items or images that tempt you away from following the voice of God. Offer a prayer for help in staying attentive to the voice and call of God this season.

Your reflections—

DAY FOUR

Read Romans 1:1-7.

To become a servant of Jesus Christ, as Paul professes to be, requires obedience. *Obedience* is based on the Greek verb that means "to hear." So, to become obedient, we must hear something; we must be told something to do or to be or to believe. Paul has heard the "gospel of God," the good news of God made known in Jesus Christ, and in a short seven verses, Paul summarizes that gospel for those who are hearing this letter.

Prayerfully reflect on who Jesus Christ is for you. Make a mental summary, or write down what you have come to believe about Jesus. What have you heard about him? Has the good news of Jesus influenced your way of living—what you do, who you are, what you believe? How? Who has told you this good news? Where have you heard it? Give God thanks for this gospel.

Your reflections—

DAY FIVE
Read Matthew 1:18-25.

IN SPITE OF the social stigma that would come from taking a wife already with child, Joseph did so. The news of Mary's pregnancy must have made his heart sink. He probably had plans and dreams for the family they would have together. The outrageous story she told him about how she had conceived must have shattered his tender trust in this young girl about to become his wife. He had heard enough and was about to say no to Mary. Yet deep within, Joseph was able to listen for another word about Mary, about himself, and about what God needed them to do. And from that deep listening, that deep prayerful place of "obedience," Joseph changed his mind and his answer. His Advent no became an Advent yes.

When have you said no to God at first but later responded yes? What changed your mind? Did your yes lead you to act in a different way? Consider whether any invitation presents itself now in your faith journey. How are you responding? Have you said yes, or have you been saying no despite a nudging toward yes? What might come of a yes to this invitation, your obedience to what God asks of you? Offer your thoughts to God and listen for a word of encouragement toward faithful obedience.

Your reflections—

DAY SIX
The Waiting World

FROM A PRACTICAL perspective, obedience is about doing what we are told to do. Practicing obedience as a spiritual discipline calls for a rhythm of regularly being obedient, of making room to listen for and act on what we are told to do on an ongoing and persistent basis. During the remainder of this season of Advent and into the season of Christmas, make a regular practice of listening to the needs of the creation by attending to a daily news source. Commit to this practice. If you already listen and read the news with the intent of hearing God's call, add a time of prayer before and after each news report or reading. A prayer could be as simple as: *Creator God, help me to have eyes to see, ears to hear, and a heart to hold your world with you. Amen.*

Prepare yourself before listening or reading by shifting into an attitude of prayer: close your eyes for a moment; take a long, slow breath in and out; then listen to or read the news. Attend to the needs of creation as presented in the news—of people, places, and circumstances—with an ear attuned to how God hears these needs. Afterward, pray for creation and for the new creation about to be born through the coming of Christ.

Your reflections—

D/AY SEVEN

Praying in Obedience

It is good to give thanks to the Lord,
  to sing praises to your name, O Most High;
to declare your steadfast love in the morning,
  and your faithfulness by night.

—Psalm 92:2

A DAILY OFFICE

There may be no better prayer practice to begin a new Christian year than a *daily office*. A daily routine for prayer, something simple, predictable, on a set rhythm and schedule can cultivate a deep practice of obedience: of listening for and hearing God's presence in the daily. The root of the word *obedience* means just this—to hear. The intent of practicing a daily office is to spend disciplined time with God, showing up at a set time alone or in community, so that a habit of prayer is established.

A daily office, often called *praying the hours*, is a set rhythm and format of prayer by which a community or individual goes obediently to God in prayer at regular intervals during the day. It might include simply morning and evening prayer; a schedule of morning, midday, and evening prayer; or a more extended daily office with as many as nine prayer times such as those practiced in many monastic orders. The time of each office should be consistently observed, even if practiced in solitude, because the rhythm and obedience of the practice are as much gifts as the content.

The content of a daily office can vary according to design by the individual or community. Most often a daily office includes a rhythm of silence, reading the psalms and other scriptures, the Lord's Prayer, along with prayers of praise, petition, and intercession, all framed by an invocation and benediction. But in fact a daily office can be as simple as coming to prayer in silence, reading a Psalm, and prayers of gratitude and petition once a day.

How better to greet Immanuel, God-With-Us, in the new year than by daily practicing to be-with-God? May this rhythm of prayer, begun in Advent, help us "hear" God daily.

A GUIDE TO THE PRACTICE OF A DAILY OFFICE

If your group or community can commit to this practice during Advent, I urge you to. Although an individual daily office opens up life with God in new ways, a communal commitment—even if just for a season, a week, or a few days—provides a particular blessing. Either way, alone or with friends, the practice will be a gift.

First determine the hours you will be in prayer. A morning and evening schedule is a good starting place. Arrange the times to accommodate your other practices and schedule. You may decide to have morning prayer at 7:00 AM or at 10:00 AM and to have afternoon or evening prayer at 4:00 PM or at 7:00 PM. If practicing alone, you might try a daily rhythm of morning, midday, and evening prayer. Again, the rhythm of your daily office can be determined by you or your group, but it is important to choose times you can observe each day over the period in which you will try this prayer practice. Part of the experience is the daily return to the same time and place to meet God and one another.

If your group wants to experience a daily office but cannot meet together, consider designing a schedule in which each person practices independently at the same times of day. For example, while at home or work, you and your friends could be in prayer at 6:00 AM, noon, and 5:30 PM each day individually, together. Knowing others are in prayer with you, even when apart, can be a powerful experience.

Whether in solitude or with a group, the format can be simple. Use a prayer book as your guide (see Resources for possibilities), or design your office according to the pattern on the next page. For scripture readings, the Revised Common Lectionary is recommended as your guide, but you may select readings if you prefer.

- Gather in Silence and light a candle as a sign of the Light of Christ being present.
- Invocation

Morning
Let me hear of your steadfast love in the morning,
    for in you I put my trust.
Teach me the way I should go,
    for to you I lift up my soul. (Ps. 143:8)

Evening
If I say, "Surely the darkness shall cover me,
    and the light around me become night,"
even the darkness is not dark to you;
    the night is as bright as the day,
    for darkness is as light to you. (Ps. 139:11-12)

- Read a Psalm
- Silence
- Read a scripture passage
- Silence
- Prayers of petition and intercession (an open time for prayers) followed by the Lord's Prayer (in unison)
- Blessing

Morning
May the love and light of God go with you into this new day. Amen.

Evening
May the Spirit of God embrace you this night in ways that bring you peace. Amen.

CHRISTMAS EVE

INVOCATION

O Holy Night,
that deepening darkness above and around,
light-pierced and silence-shrouded,
out of which little children are called in
and seeking shepherds are sent out.
O night of nights,
you spread across heaven
and touch the earth,
surrounding God's people,
capturing us in a moment of holy time,
like a globe protects a precious flicker of Light.
Come,
draw us in,
hold us together
while we wait for the birth of the Light of lights,
the One who will guide us into the world anew. Amen.

GUIDE FOR SMALL GROUPS

THIS RESOURCE CAN be shared by two friends, a small group, or even a Sunday school class who desire to move through the season of Advent together. The materials can be adapted for a forty-five-minute gathering up to a two-hour session. The basic pattern for facilitating a group conversation each week can be found in the materials for Day One of each week, all of which can be adapted or supplemented by readings from any of the other days. A group's facilitator will not need to spend more than thirty additional minutes beyond the preparation time of all group participants. That individual will need to prepare to guide the group through the session by selecting the elements for each gathering. Facilitation for a group can be shared by different members of the group.

FOR THE FACILITATOR

Be sure that all participants know where, when, and how long the group will meet so they feel fully prepared and informed. Each participant will need a copy of *Simply Wait*, preferably at least one full week in advance of the first session. Also it is helpful to remind group participants to bring a Bible and, if desired, a journal.

Select a setting for the gathering that is conducive to conversation. It could be a classroom, living room, or other comfortable setting. Set up the space so people will be able to see and hear one another easily. Lighting Advent candles would be appropriate for the beginning of each session as a time of quieting and prayer and to underscore the ongoing nature of the season. Advent candles can be purchased in Christian book and supply stores in your community, online at www.cokesbury.com, or from other denominational outlets.

Schedule the four Advent gatherings to conclude as close to Christmas as possible for your group. It does not matter which day of the week you choose; any day will do.

Preparation for facilitating a group or class conversation involves two basic steps:

1. Read through all of the materials for the week, making personal notes and reflections just as all participants will do.
2. Choose which exercises to use in your gathering based on the length of time your class or group will meet.

If your group decides to learn and participate in the weekly Advent prayer practice together, the facilitator also needs to take responsibility for organizing that component. Some practices may require additional group time to practice together (such as vigils and a daily office). Instructions for each prayer practice are included in the weekly material.

Materials Needed

Copies of *Simply Wait* for all participants; candle or Advent candles; chalkboard, dry-erase board, or flip chart; Bible.

Guiding the Group

• At the first gathering welcome everyone and ask individuals to introduce themselves if participants do not know one another.

• Take a few moments to set the tone for these gatherings and conversations by summarizing these understandings or ground rules for your time together:

~ Everyone will arrive on time, and the session will end on time.

~ These gatherings constitute a safe place where confidentiality will be honored.

~ We will give each other room to speak and practice listening without needing to analyze, clarify, or respond.

~ No one needs to feel compelled to speak or share. We will honor the presence and practice of silence.

~ We will arrange for breaks as needed.

• Once all have arrived, invite people to settle into the space and to enter into a few moments of quiet. If you use Advent candles, light them at this point. (two to five minutes)

- Write on the board or chart in large letters the word of the week. Invite the group to share reaction and response to the word, using the questions from Day One to guide the conversation. Do not hurry this response time. It is, in its own way, a call to worship for the gathering. (ten to twenty minutes)
- Pray the invocation for the week together. Lead the speaking with a slow pace, listening to the words. (one minute)
- Return to silence, and do not rush this period. (two to five minutes)
- (Optional) Sing or read the hymn for the week in preparation for the Word. (two to three minutes)
- Now invite a conversation around one or all of the scripture reflections for the week. You can be very flexible in the time allotted to this segment of the group session. (fifteen to sixty minutes).

   - If your group is meeting for an hour or less you could simply ask which passages or reflections caught their attention in particular ways. Another option is to read one scripture aloud, possibly the Gospel text for the week, and invite the whole group to work through the reflection for that reading together. (fifteen minutes)

   - If your group has a longer session together, you could read each passage aloud and spend time in the reflection. (fifteen minutes on each: sixty minutes)

- (Optional) If your group wants to explore the Advent prayer practice as part of this study, this is the time to begin a conversation around the practice of the week. Some may not have chosen to try the practice, while others may have experienced it. Spend a few minutes introducing or reminding participants about the practice of the week. Invite both reactions to the prayer form as well as personal experiences with it. If, after the conversation, there is interest in a group practice, set another time in which to participate together. (ten to twenty minutes)
- Take time to reflect together on A Waiting World from Day Six. Read the reflection and ask for responses. Keep a focus on the word of the week in this conversation. This will communicate a

deep intentionality to connect the word with the world. If you need to, point back to the word of the week written on the board or chart. (ten to twenty minutes)

If the group names an action they can take together out of this reflection, encourage that action.

• Before departing, ask one person to read the Benediction.

GUIDE FOR AN ADVENT RETREAT

An Advent time apart could be designed around any one or all of these words and sessions. Think "simplicity" in planning your time apart. Make room for much silence and for participants to be able to use their imaginations. Whatever the length of the retreat, keep the focus of each session on a single Advent word that you have selected (Anticipation, Hope, Patience, or Obedience). If your retreat will have time to focus on only one of these words, you may either select the word according to the lectionary readings for the week of your retreat or select the word that catches your attention and Advent imagination.

For a Half Day Apart
Select one word out of the four Advent words as your focus. Begin the day with a simple worship time using the Invocation and *Hymn* from the Advent week's material. Incorporate silence and a scripture reading for reflection. Then send retreatants into a time of silence. Instruct them to spend this time with the chosen word and the questions around the word. Follow with a group session in which people can share insights from that experience. A closing time of prayer and worship ends the retreat.

For a Full Day Apart
On a full-day retreat, spend the morning as described above (Half Day Apart), followed by a shared meal. In the afternoon, guide retreatants into the prayer practice included in the session you have chosen, first individually and then as a group experience. Close with prayers of the people and your word's Day One Benediction.

For an Overnight Retreat

The additional time available on an overnight retreat could allow sessions based on all four Advent words and prayer practices (Anticipation, Hope, Patience, and Obedience), or you might select only one word and session based on the lectionary readings for the week of your retreat.

If your retreat focuses on a single word and session, your opening session will be based on Day One; your second session will center on one or two of the scripture readings and reflections that you, as leader, have selected; and your closing session can be framed by the prayer practice to be experienced as a group.

If your retreat is designed to include all four words from *Simply Wait*, the following framework can be your guide:

FIRST EVENING SESSION

Gather. Present the theme of *Simply Wait* (use Introduction).
Use Day One material for *Anticipation* (one hour).

> Invite participants to reflect silently on the word, using the questions on pages 18–20 (thirty minutes). Conclude by praying the Invocation in unison. Then read the Reflection on pages 21–22 aloud and talk about *Anticipation*, guided by questions on pages 18–20 (twenty minutes). Pray the Benediction in unison.

Prepare for practice of Vigils in the morning (see pages 35–37).

FIRST MORNING SESSION

Observe Vigils together as morning prayer.
Breakfast and Break

Use Day One material for *Hope* (one hour).

Select one scripture reading and reflection from the week on *Hope* (thirty minutes of individual silent reflection, followed by a twenty-minute group sharing).

Introduce Daily Examen to be practiced this evening before bed.

Lunch
Allow at least two hours following lunch for rest and relaxation.

Use Day One material for *Patience* (one hour).

Select one scripture reading and reflection from the week on *Patience* (thirty minutes of individual silent reflection, followed by a twenty-minute group sharing).

Introduce The Jesus Prayer (see pages 79–81).

Dinner

This is an informal time together. Gather for conversation about the day, the season, and the prayers.

Sing hymns of the season.

Include free time for group reflection and discussion.

Review the Daily Examen.

Individuals will practice the Daily Examen before bed.

Offer a brief introduction to a daily office using pages 101–103 (ten minutes). Use the pattern on page 103 to lead the group in a morning daily office (twenty minutes). Remember to select the Psalm and scripture in advance.

Break to prepare for departure

Close with a simple worship that includes time for sharing and for prayer. Conclude worship by inviting different voices to read each of the four benedictions from *Simply Wait* (found on pages 23, 45, 67, 89).

RESOURCES

Find lectionary readings at www.gbod.org/worship/lectionary

Dawson, Gerrit Scott; Adele Gonzalez, E. Glenn Hinson, Rueben P. Job, Marjorie J.Thompson, and Wendy M. Wright, *Companions in Christ: A Small-Group Experience in Spiritual Formation. Participant's Book.* Nashville, Tenn.: Upper Room Books, 2001.

Foster, Richard J. *Prayer: Finding the Heart's True Home.* New York: HarperCollins, 1992.

Funk, Mary Margaret. *Tools Matter for Practicing the Spiritual Life.* New York: Continuum, 2001.

Job, Rueben P., and Norman Shawchuck. *A Guide to Prayer for All God's People.* Nashville, Tenn.: Upper Room Books, 1990.

Job, Rueben P., and Norman Shawchuck. *A Guide to Prayer for All Who Seek God.* Nashville: Upper Room Books, 2003.

Killinger, John. *Beginning Prayer.* Rev. ed. Nashville, Tenn.: Upper Room Books, 1995.

Newell, J. Philip. *Celtic Prayers from Iona.* Mahwah, N.J.: Paulist Press, 1997.

Rowlett, Martha Graybeal. *Praying Together: Forming Prayer Ministries in Your Congregation.* Nashville, Tenn.: Upper Room Books, 2002.

Thompson, Marjorie J. *Soul Feast: An Invitation to the Christian Spiritual Life.* Louisville, Ky.: Westminster John Knox Press, 1995.

StillPoint Programs in Spiritual Direction and Contemplative Prayer directed by Dr. Kathleen R. Flood, OP. Nashville, TN. www.stillpointnashville.org

ABOUT THE AUTHOR

PAMELA C. HAWKINS serves as associate pastor of Belle Meade United Methodist Church in Nashville, Tennessee. Previously she held positions at Duke Divinity School, as associate director of the Duke Center for Excellence in Ministry, and Upper Room Ministries, as associate editor of *Weavings*.

CPSIA information can be obtained
at www.ICGtesting.com
Printed in the USA
LVOW04s0740211016

509325LV00004BA/6/P